UNDERSTANDING DISEASE AND WELLNESS

Kids' Guides to Why People Get Sick and How They Can Stay Well

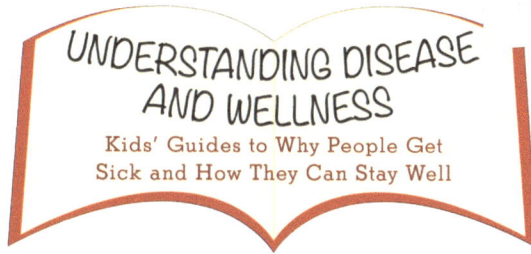

A KID'S GUIDE TO AIDS & HIV

VILLAGE EARTH PRESS

Series List

A KID'S GUIDE TO A HEALTHIER YOU

A KID'S GUIDE TO AIDS AND HIV

A KID'S GUIDE TO ALLERGIES

A KID'S GUIDE TO ASTHMA

A KID'S GUIDE TO BUGS AND HOW THEY CAN MAKE YOU SICK

A KID'S GUIDE TO CANCER

A KID'S GUIDE TO DIABETES

A KID'S GUIDE TO DRUGS AND ALCOHOL

A KID'S GUIDE TO IMMUNIZATIONS

A KID'S GUIDE TO MALNUTRITION

A KID'S GUIDE TO OBESITY

A KID'S GUIDE TO POLLUTION AND HOW IT CAN MAKE YOU SICK

A KID'S GUIDE TO VIRUSES AND BACTERIA

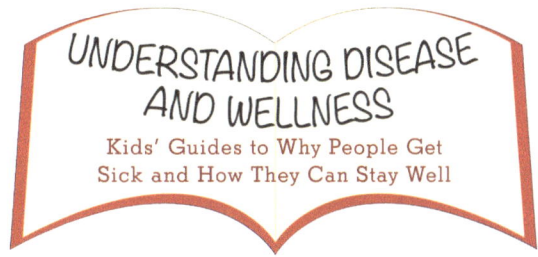

A KID'S GUIDE TO
AIDS & HIV

Rae Simons

Understanding Disease and Wellness:
Kids' Guides to Why People Get Sick and How They Can Stay Well
A KID'S GUIDE TO AIDS & HIV

Village Earth Press
Vestal, New York 13850
www.villageearthpress.com

First Printing
9 8 7 6 5 4 3 2 1

Series ISBN (paperback): 978-1-62524-445-1
ISBN (paperback): 978-1-62524-410-9
ebook ISBN: 978-1-62524-045-3

Library of Congress Control Number: 2013911238

Author: Simons, Rae

Note: This book is a revised and updated edition of *AIDS & HIV: The Facts for Kids* (ISBN: 978-1-934970-20-1), published in 2009 by Alpha House Publishing.

Introduction

According to a recent study reported in the Virginia Henderson International Nursing Library, kids worry about getting sick. They worry about AIDS and cancer, about allergies and the "super-germs" that resist medication. They know about these ills—but they don't always understand what causes them or how they can be prevented.

Unfortunately, most 9- to 11-year-olds, the study found, get their information about diseases like AIDS from friends and television; only 20 percent of the children interviewed based their understanding of illness on facts they had learned at school. Too often, kids believe urban legends, schoolyard folktales, and exaggerated movie plots. Oftentimes, misinformation like this only makes their worries worse. The January 2008 *Child Health News* reported that 55 percent of all children between 9 and 13 "worry almost all the time" about illness.

This series, **Understanding Disease and Wellness**, offers readers clear information on various illnesses and conditions, as well as the immunizations that can prevent many diseases. The books dispel the myths with clearly presented facts and colorful, accurate illustrations. Better yet, these books will help kids understand not only illness—but also what they can do to stay as healthy as possible.

—*Dr. Elise Berlan*

Just the Facts

- HIV (Human Immunodeficiency Virus) is the germ that causes the sickness called AIDS (Acquired Immunodeficiency Syndrome).

- HIV hurts your immune system so it can't fight off germs. Some of these germs wouldn't even hurt you if you didn't have HIV.

- You can get HIV from body fluids—by using a needle that was used by someone with HIV, or by having unprotected sex with a person who has the virus. HIV can also be passed from mother to child.

- You cannot get AIDS by giving blood, being touched by or breathed on by a person with AIDS, or touching things a person with AIDS touched. The only way you catch it is from body fluids.

- HIV can often be in a person's body for years before anyone knows.

- The only way to be sure you have AIDS is to be tested by a doctor.

- Scientists have found ways to help people live for years with AIDS. However, scientists are still looking for new treatments, as well as a vaccine for the disease.

- Although AIDS is a problem around the world, it is worst in Africa and Asia, where many people don't have enough money to pay for treatment for the disease.

What Is AIDS?

You hear a lot about AIDS and HIV these days. You may have seen television shows and movies where characters had this disease. You might hear about it at school. You may even know someone who has it. You may think it has to do somehow with homosexuals. But lots of kids—and adults, too—don't really understand what HIV/AIDS is. They don't know how you catch it, who gets it, or what causes it. Lots of people don't even know what these letters stand for: **A**cquired **I**mmuno**D**eficiency *Syndrome*—**AIDS**—got its name because:

It is **acquired**; in other words, it's something that has to be passed to you from another person. It is not handed down to you through your genes; it cannot be passed down to you from your parents. This means

Words to Know

Syndrome: a collection of symptoms doctors don't completely understand.

if your boyfriend has AIDS you could catch it from him—but if your grandmother who lives in another country has AIDS, you're not going to discover that she passed it on to you.

It changes the body's immune system, the part of the body that fights off diseases.

It is called a deficiency because it makes the immune system stop working the way it should.

At first doctors thought it was a syndrome (and not a disease) because people with AIDS have a number of different symptoms and diseases.

What Is HIV?

Today, doctors think that "HIV disease" is a better name for AIDS. HIV stands for **H**uman **I**mmunodeficiency *Virus*. It's the virus that causes AIDS. People can have the HIV virus (shown here) inside their bodies, but not seem sick.

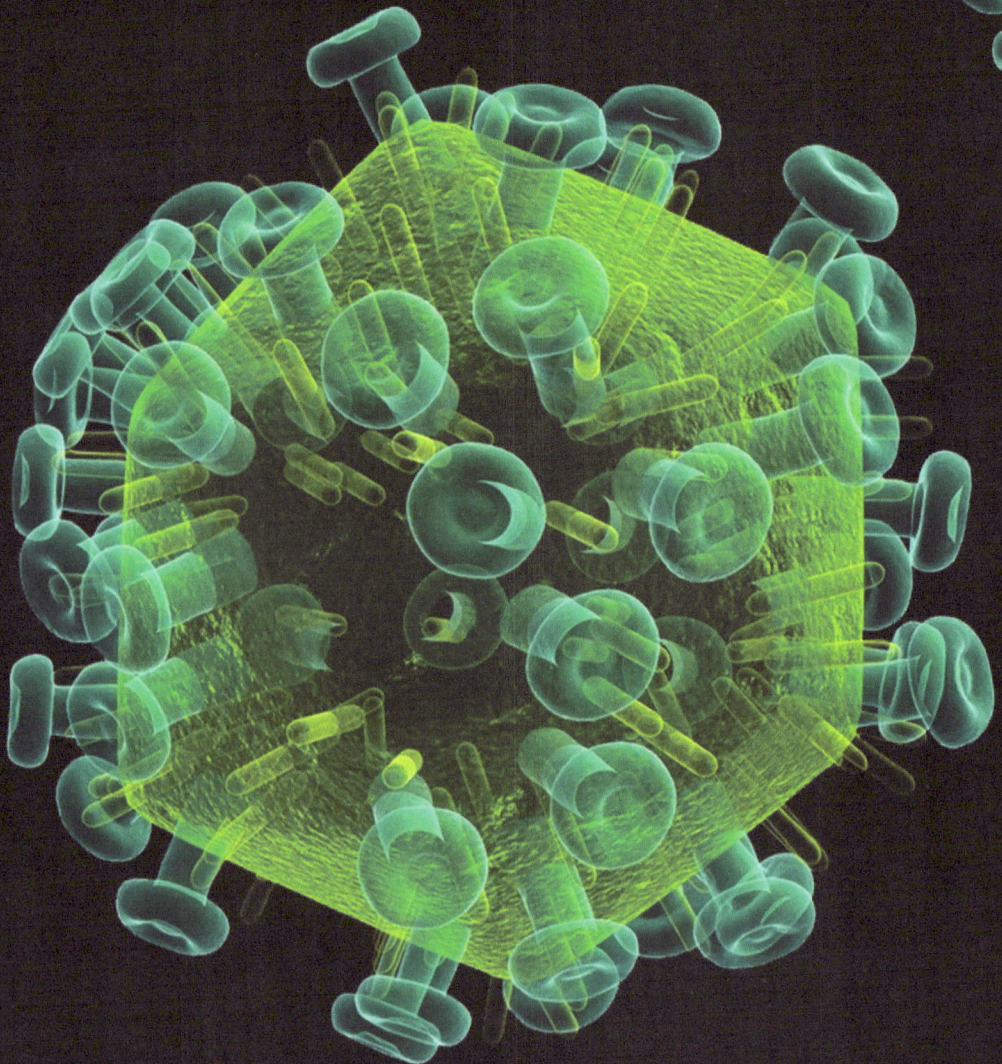

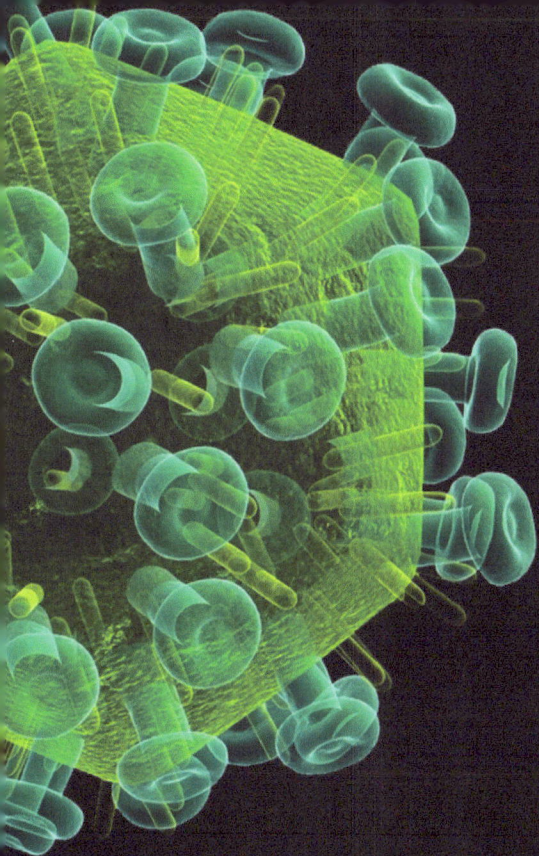

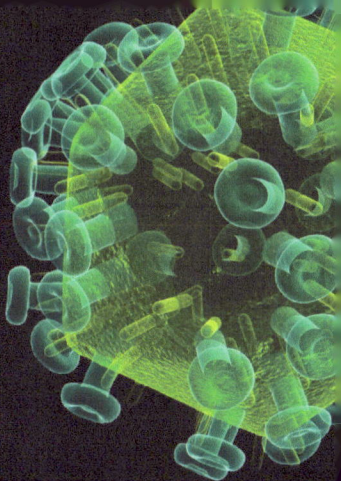

As the disease becomes worse, though, and people develop symptoms, it often is called HIV disease—or AIDS.

Words to Know

Virus: a very tiny germ that can only grow by getting inside a living cell.

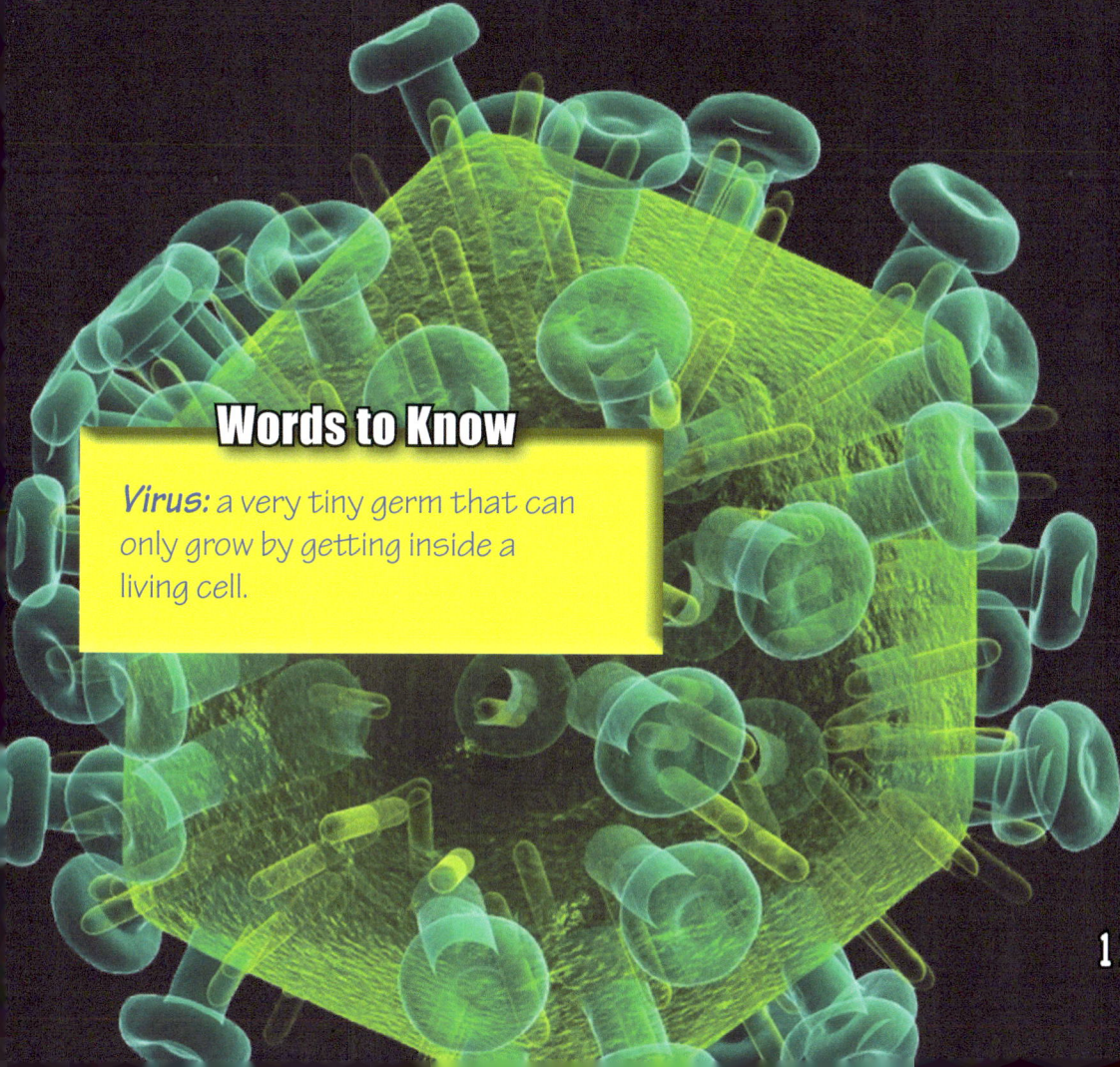

Where Did HIV/AIDS Come From?

Scientists believe that HIV began in chimpanzees in Africa. The virus was probably spread to humans when people killed the chimpanzees for their meat. Blood from the animals got into the hunters' wounds—and the first people caught the virus. Scientists and doctors gave HIV/AIDS its name in the 1980s when the first people started getting sick with it. At first, many patients were *homosexual* men—which made some people think this was a "homosexual problem."

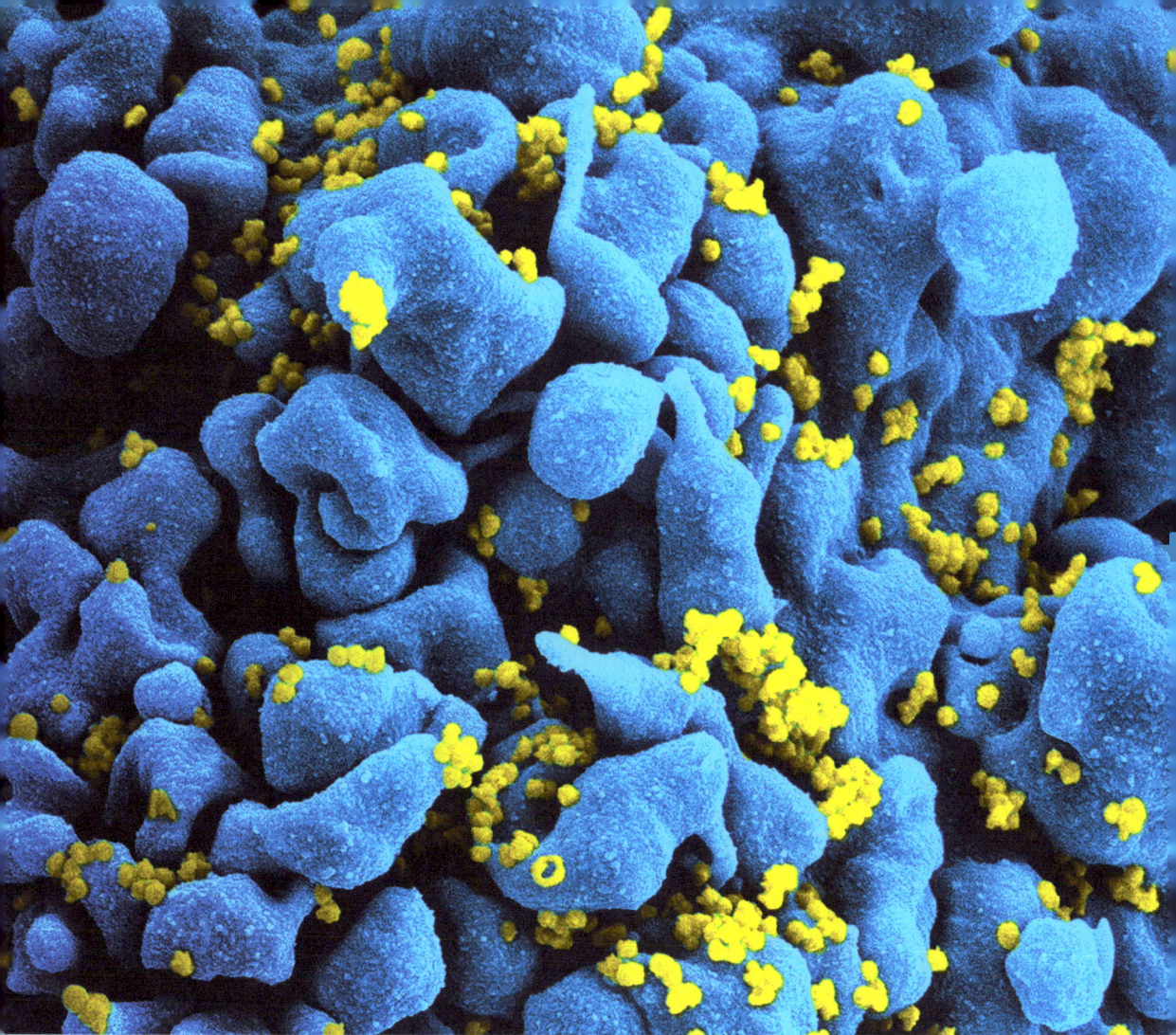

Words to Know

Homosexual: a person who wants to have sex with a member of the same sex. Male homosexuals are attracted to males, female homosexuals to females.

Before long, doctors realized other people were getting sick with HIV and AIDS, too. Doctors know now that AIDS is an "everybody" problem. Anyone can catch the viruses shown magnified many thousands of times in the photo above.

13

What Does HIV/AIDS Do Inside Your Body?

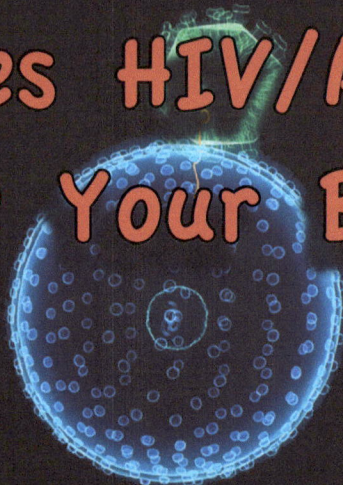

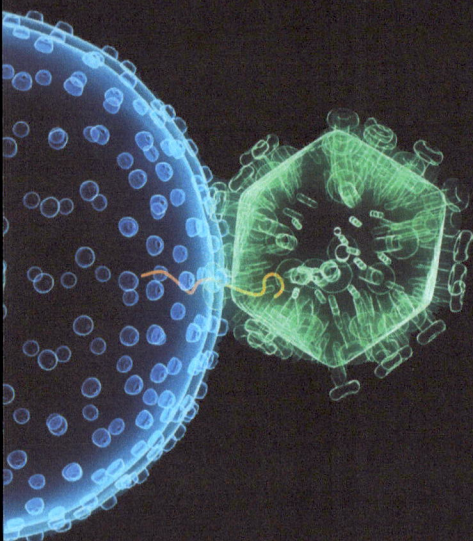

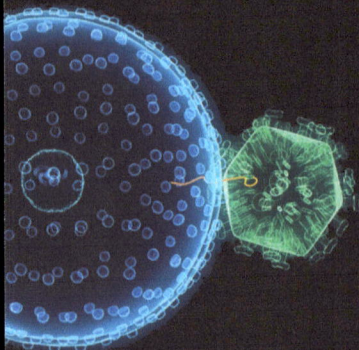

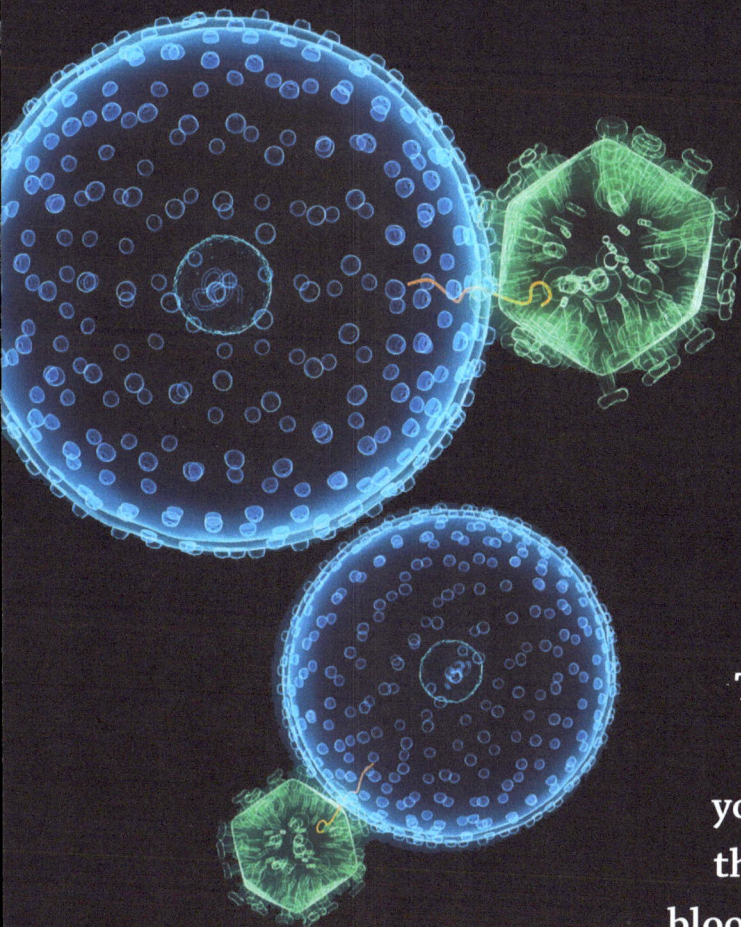

The worst thing about AIDS is that it hurts your immune system— the special cells in your blood that fight off germs and keep you from getting sick. In this picture, the green shapes are HIV viruses attacking the body's healthy cells (the blue circles). When this happens, your body isn't able to fight off germs, and you can get sick with other things. People with AIDS often die from another disease (such as *pneumonia* or cancer).

How Your Body Fights HIV

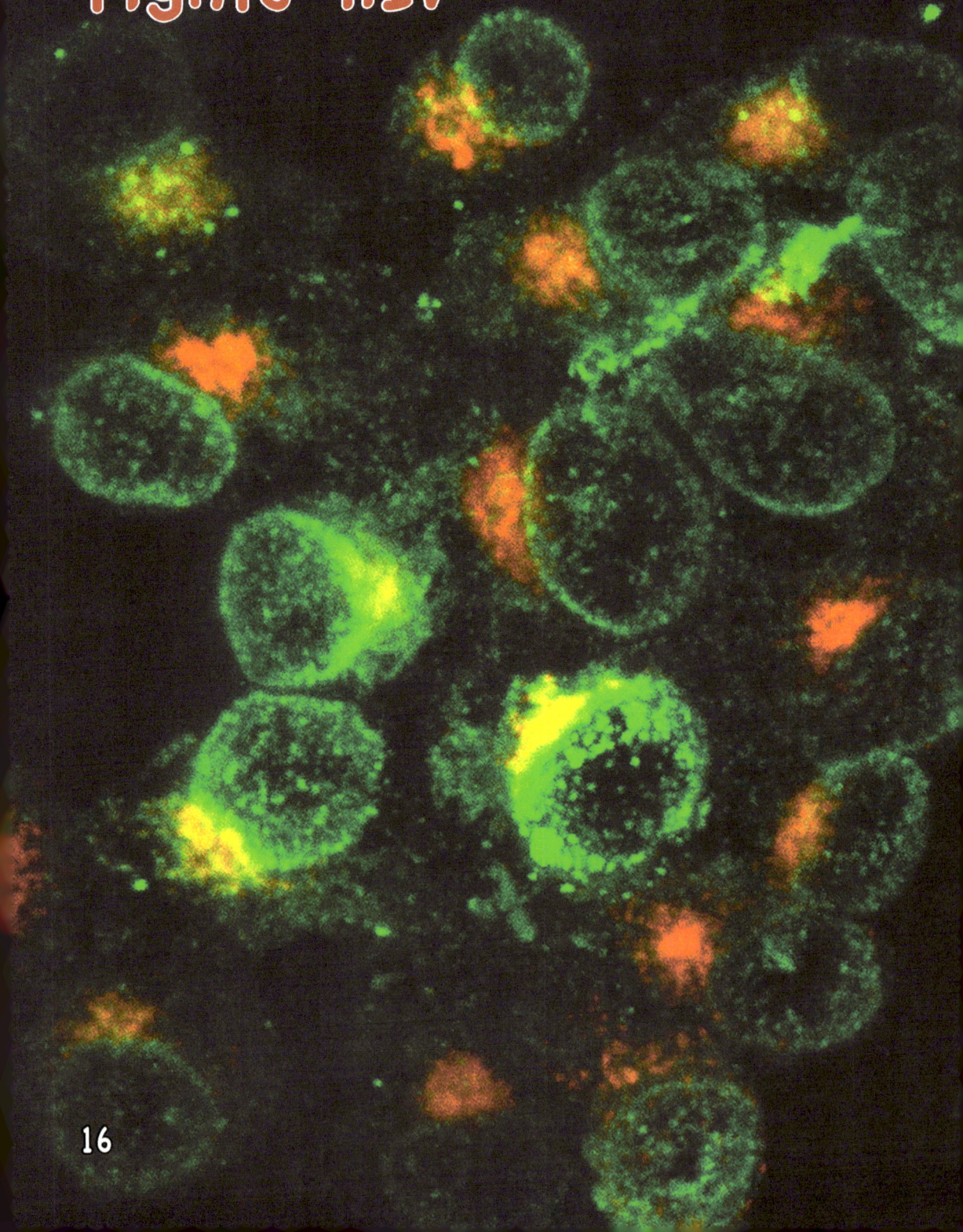

When a virus or bacteria (what we often call germs) gets into your body through a cut, through the air you breathe, or through something you've eaten, special cells in your blood—white blood cells called helper T cells—get busy. They pass along the message to another group of white blood cells—B cells—telling them to make the weapons (called antibodies) they need to kill the germs. If a virus or bacteria makes its way past the antibodies, it can cause an infection. When that happens, a different type of T cell recognizes the change in the infected cell and kills it (as shown in the picture to the left). This prevents the infection from spreading. At least this is what is *supposed* to happen. But when someone has HIV, eventually she will no longer be able to fight off infections that other people have no problem fighting off.

How Do You Catch HIV/AIDS?

First of all, here are ways you CAN'T catch AIDS:

You can't catch AIDS from being in the same room with someone who has HIV/AIDS.

You can't catch AIDS from touching something that someone with HIV/AIDS has touched.

You can't catch AIDS from breathing the same air as someone with HIV/AIDS.

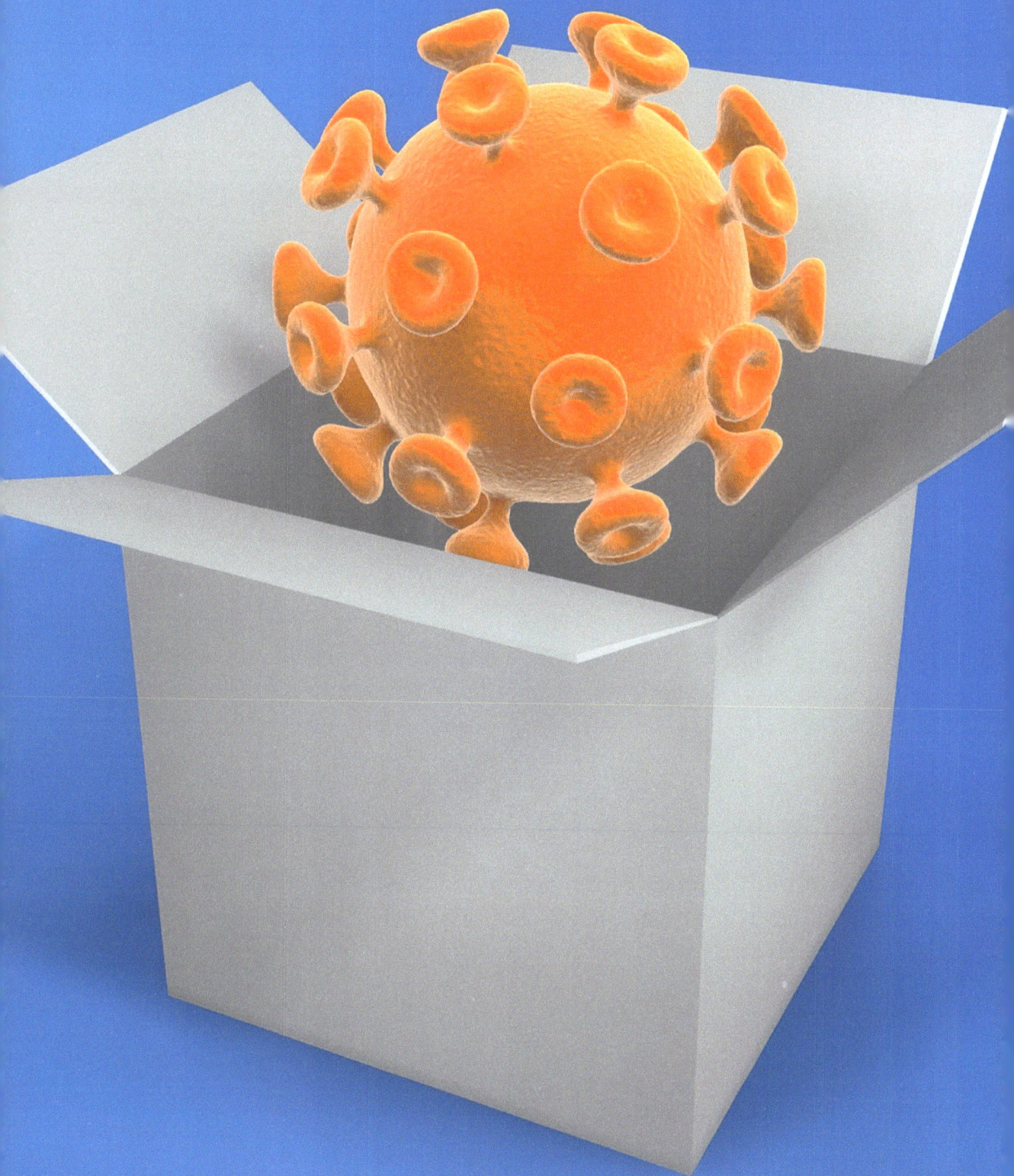

The ONLY way to catch HIV/AIDS is through certain body fluids.

Sex

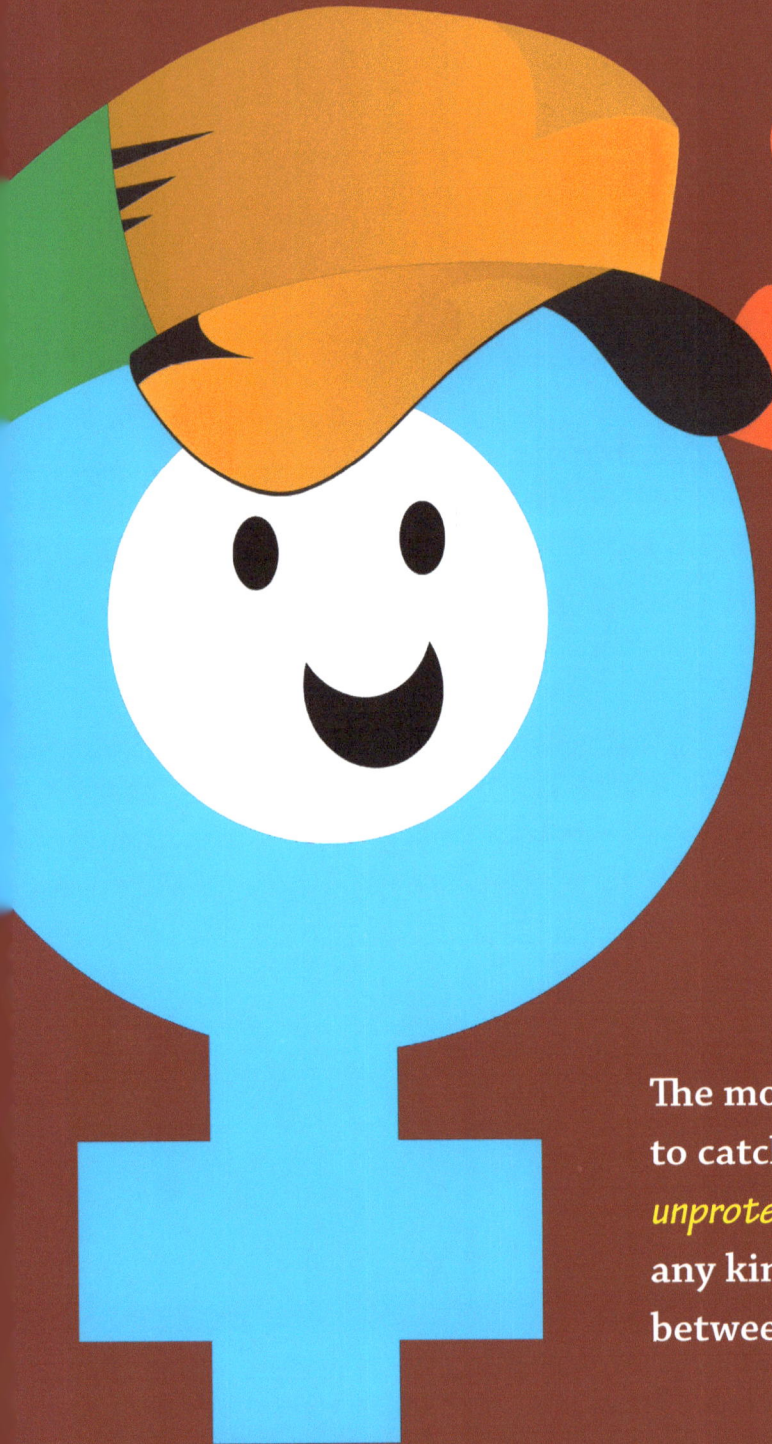

The most common way to catch HIV is through *unprotected sex*. This means any kind of sex, not just sex between two homosexuals.

Words to Know

Unprotected sex: when people have sex with each other without using a condom or other protection. A condom is like a tight rubber glove that fits over the man's penis and keeps his semen—the fluid that comes out of his penis when he has sex—from getting out.

Blood

Words to Know

Donors: people who give something. A blood donor gives his blood so people who are hurt or sick can use it.

Hemophilia: an illness in which blood clots much more slowly than normal. As a result, small cuts and other injuries cause heavy bleeding. Boys are more likely to have this disease than girls.

In the 1970s and early 1980s, before anyone knew very much about HIV/AIDS, some blood *donors* didn't know they had the disease, so when they gave their blood to hospitals and at Red Cross blood drives, the virus got into the blood that was given out to sick or injured people.

Eventually, doctors realized that some people were catching HIV/AIDS from blood transfusions. Beginning in 1985, the blood supply has been tested for HIV, and there is no longer much risk that someone will get HIV/AIDS from a blood transfusion. However, people who received transfusions between 1975 and 1985 had a high risk of getting the infected blood. Among the people most at risk are those with *hemophilia*. People with hemophilia use blood to control bleeding episodes. Between 1975 and 1985, as many as half the people with hemophilia caught HIV through blood.

Dirty Drug Needles

Some drug users put drugs into their veins with a hypodermic needle like the one shown here. Hypodermic needles cost money, and drug users often spend most of their money on drugs. They don't want to spend money on needles, so they often share them.

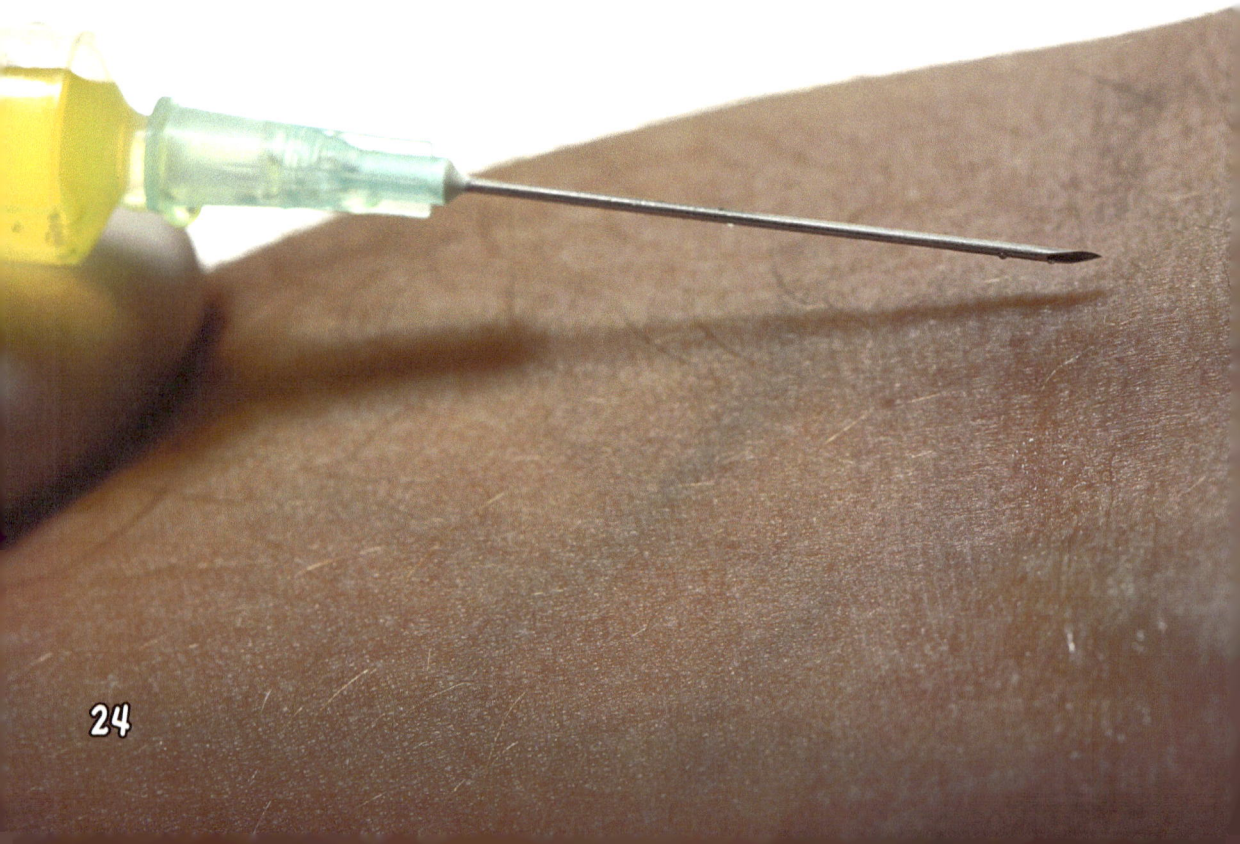

When drug users share needles, some blood from the last user often stays on the used needle. If that person had HIV in his blood, the next person to use the needle will be injecting the virus along with the drug into his blood. This makes *intravenous* drug users another group of people who are at high risk of catching HIV/AIDS.

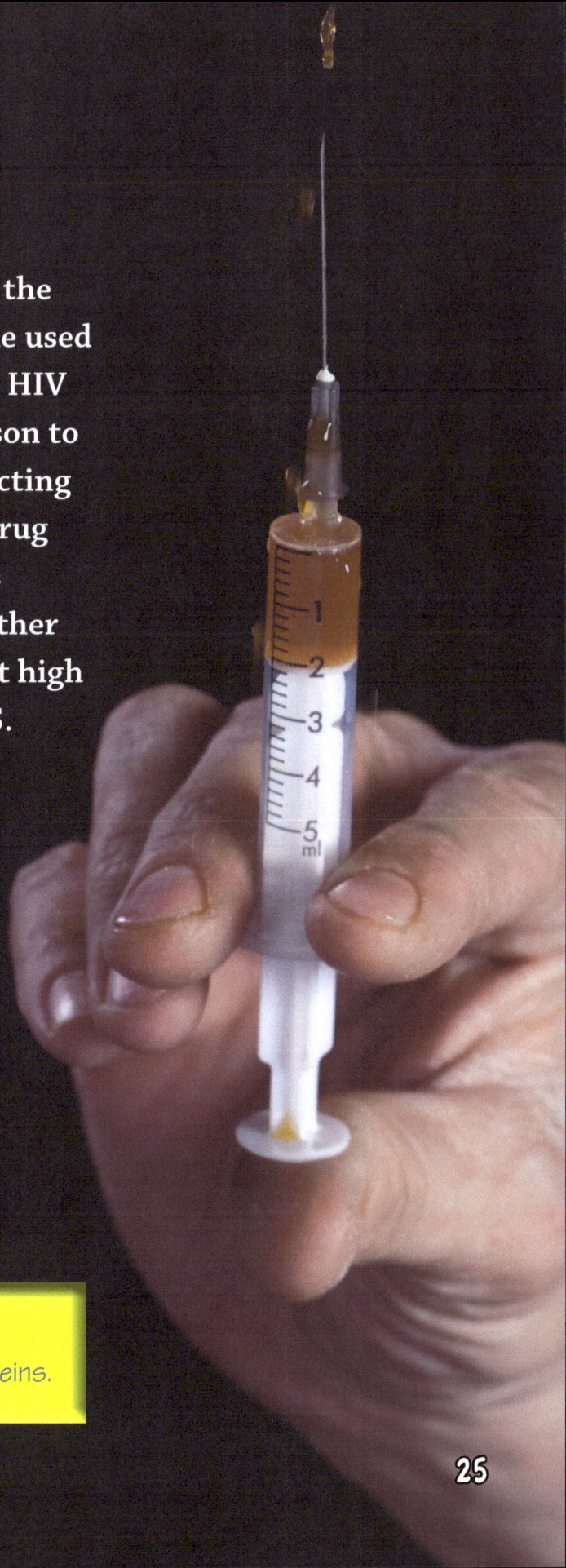

Words to Know

Intravenous: having to do with something that goes into the veins.

Mother to Child

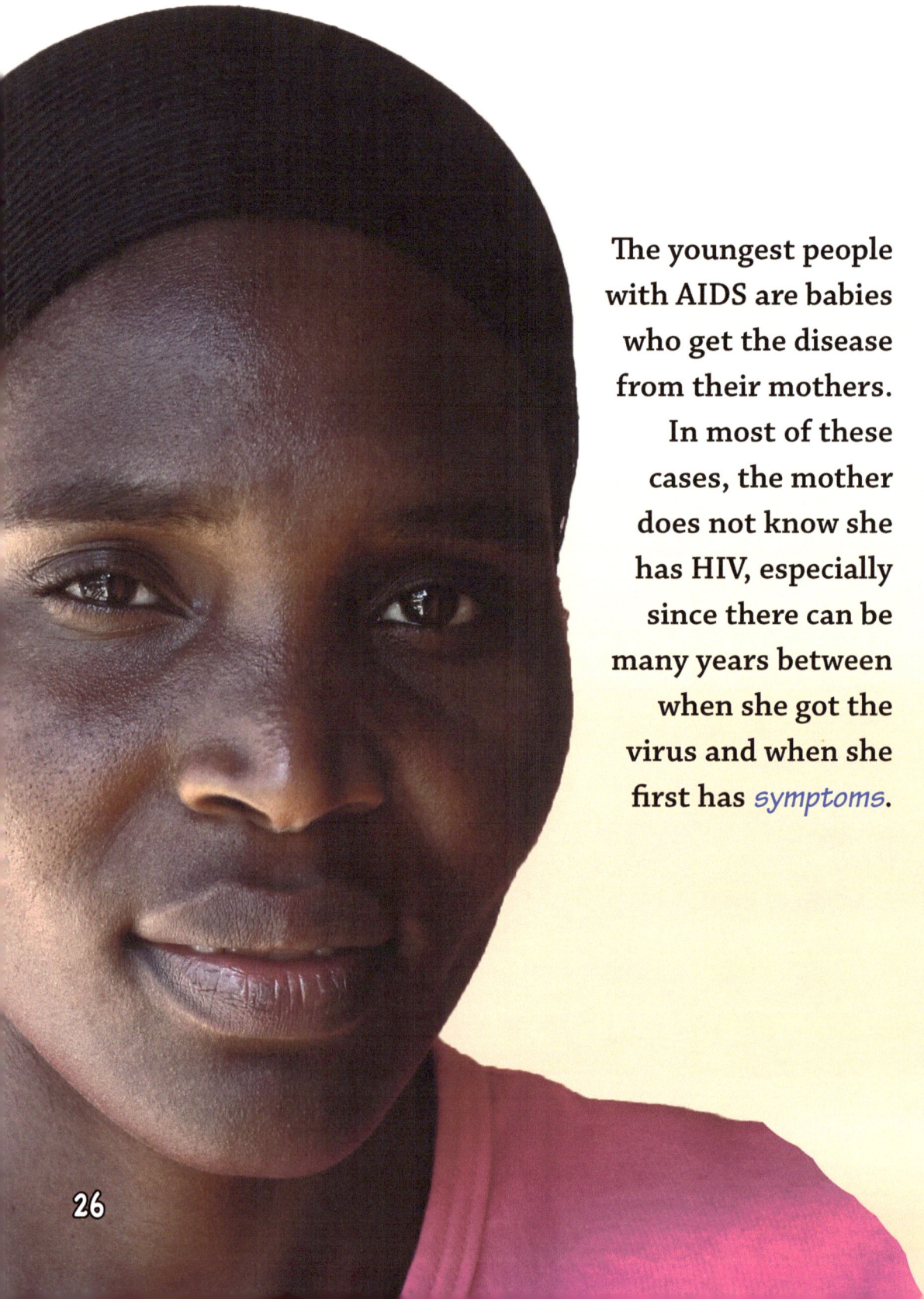

The youngest people with AIDS are babies who get the disease from their mothers. In most of these cases, the mother does not know she has HIV, especially since there can be many years between when she got the virus and when she first has *symptoms*.

If there is any chance a woman could have caught HIV, she should be tested for the virus before becoming pregnant. Medicine can be given to pregnant women with HIV to protect their babies during pregnancy. After the baby is born, women with HIV should not breastfeed, so that the virus isn't passed to their babies through breast milk.

Words to Know

Symptoms: signs of a disease. Symptoms could be a fever, a rash, a pain, or anything else that can be seen or felt that's caused by a disease.

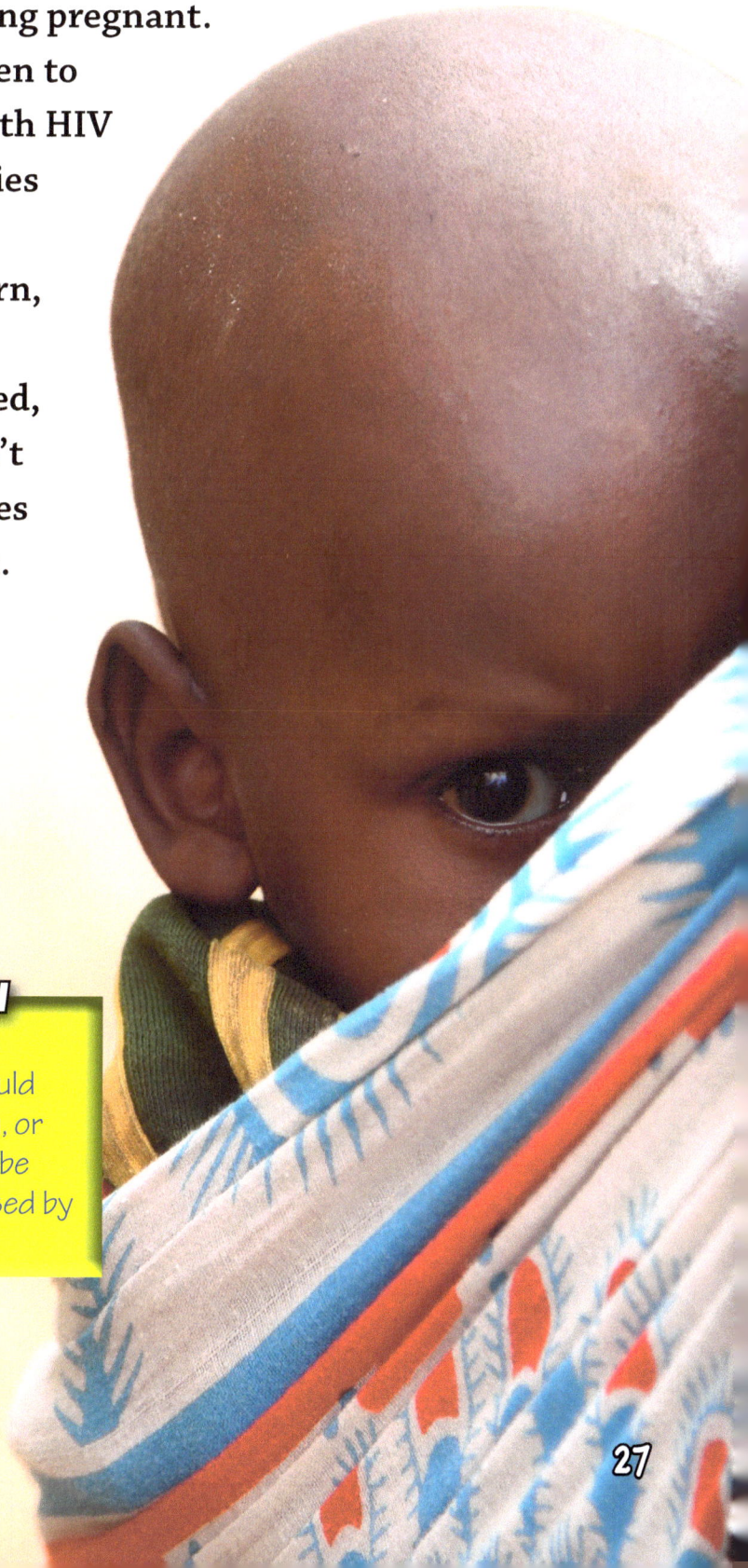

Dirty Tattoo Equipment

Tattoos are becoming more and more popular, especially among young people. But the needles used for tattooing (and also for body piercing) can carry HIV. When the needle pierces your skin to *inject* the dye, it may also be injecting HIV into your blood.

Tattoo needles need to be *disinfected* after every use. So if you decide to get a tattoo, be sure to have it done by someone who uses only clean equipment.

Words to Know

Inject: to push a fluid into something.

Disinfected: killed all germs.

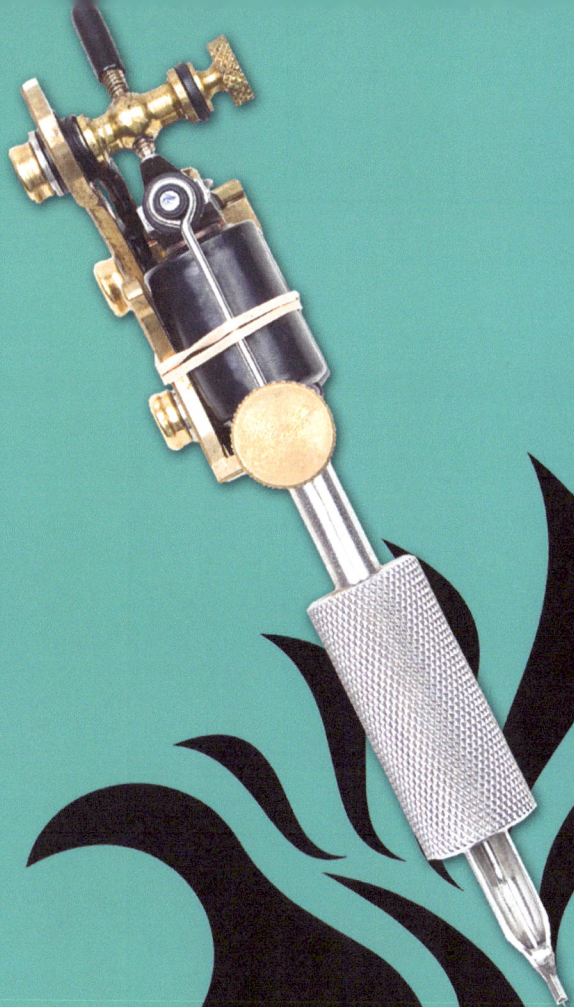

How Do You Know If You Have HIV/AIDS?

The only way to know for sure if you have HIV is to go to the doctor and get a blood test. The blood test will check to see if you have the antibodies in your blood that your body makes to fight the virus. If you do have these antibodies, it means HIV is in your blood. This means you have HIV.

ASK THE DOCTOR

My sister's friend got tested for HIV and it came back negative—but the doctor says she has to go back for another test in a few months. How come?

Answer: It takes a while for your body to create enough HIV antibodies to show up on the blood test. To be safe, doctors often ask people to come back for a second or even a third test, especially if there's a good chance the person could have caught HIV. It's better to be absolutely certain.

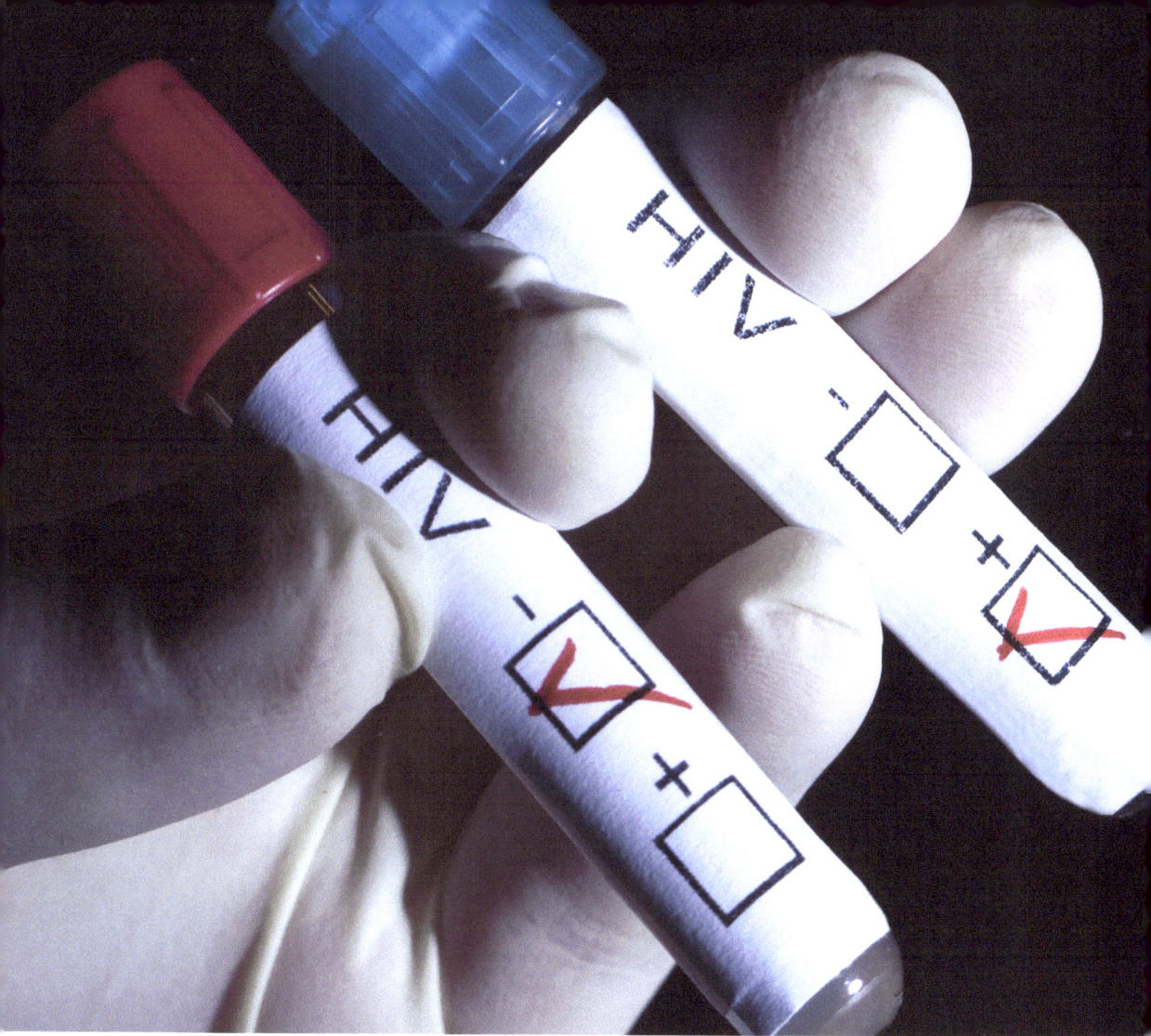

Just because you have HIV, though, doesn't mean you have AIDS. Doctors only say a person has AIDS once tests show he has HIV in his blood, he has had one or more AIDS-related infection or illness, and the number of helper T cells in his blood has fallen below a certain level.

What Happens
If You Have HIV?

Up until recently, if you found out you had HIV, you knew you would die soon. Today, however, some people who have the virus have still not developed AIDS even after many years. AIDS has no cure yet, but many people with HIV are living longer and staying healthier. New medicines have made this possible.

Treatment for HIV/AIDS

Scientists have not found a cure for AIDS yet, but they have found new and powerful drugs that allow people to stay healthy longer. For many people living with HIV/AIDS, a single medicine does not work. Most take a combination of many drugs. The drugs work together to make fewer HIV cells in the body, allowing the body's own helper T cells to grow again. This helps the person stay healthy.

Sometimes people try *alternative* medicines to fight HIV/ AIDS. St. John's Wort (the yellow flower shown above) and aloe (the green plant to the right) may help strengthen the immune system. Acupuncture (needles stuck into the skin, as shown here) can also help some of the symptoms of AIDS.

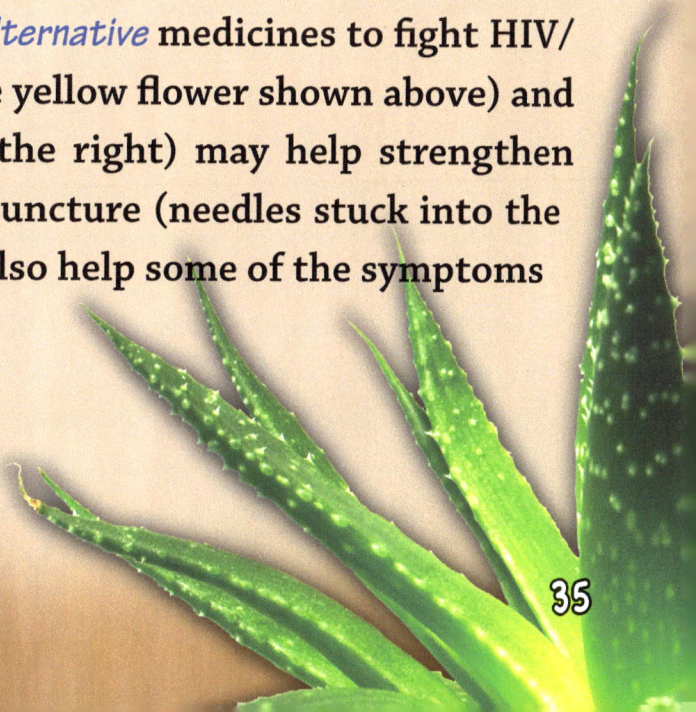

What Is HIV/ AIDS Doing to the World?

The big problem with the medicines used to treat AIDS is that they cost a lot. Around the world, many of the people living with HIV/AIDS are also living in poverty. They may not have money to buy the medicine or even go to the doctor. They may live in a country so poor that they don't even have a doctor or clinic nearby where they could go if they did have money.

People living with HIV/AIDS in North America, Europe, and other *developed* nations have a better chance of living longer, even when they are poor. Many of these countries have special programs to help bring AIDS medicines to people.

Words to Know

Developed: countries where most of the people make more money and have all the services they need, like good roads, schools, and hospitals. There are many industries in these countries. Japan, the United States, Canada, Israel, and many of the countries in Europe are all developed countries.

North America

In North America, HIV/ AIDS is worse for blacks and other *minorities* than it is for whites.

Words to Know

Minorities: groups of people who are different from the larger group to which they belong.

AIDS is the leading cause of death for black Americans between the ages of twenty-five and forty-four.

Did You Know?

Doctors are finding between 35,000 to 40,000 new cases of HIV in the United States every year—but because of new medicines, not as many people are dying in the United States.

Africa

Did You Know?

Africa is home to just over 10 percent of the world's people, but more than 60 percent of all the people in the world living with HIV live there.

In Africa, HIV has touched the lives of more than a quarter of the people living there. This means that one of every four people either has HIV/AIDS or has a household member with the disease. Almost everyone in Africa has a neighbor, a teacher, a friend, or a relative who is sick or dying.

More than half of all the women and teenage girls in Africa have HIV/AIDS. More than 11 million children are orphans because of AIDS.

ASK THE DOCTOR

Do people in Africa get a different kind of AIDS than people in the rest of the world?

Answer: No, AIDS is always caused by HIV, and the ways HIV passes from person to person are exactly the same in all parts of the world. There may be some different strains of HIV in Africa, but the virus is pretty much the same as it is in the rest of the world. What's different about Africa is how poor it is, and how many other diseases there are. This means that people with AIDS are less likely to get the medicine they need and may run into many other germs their bodies cannot fight off.

Asia

Words to Know

Epidemic: a disease that is widespread, so that large numbers of people get sick.

Asia has been hit hard by the AIDS *epidemic*. More AIDS deaths happen here than anywhere else in the world except Africa. Russia has almost no AIDS education program at all. India is the Asian country with the most people who have HIV.

Between two and three million of the people in India are living with AIDS. Because so many people in India can't read, the government has had a hard time teaching its people how to prevent HIV. The numbers of new cases are falling now, though, because the government and other agencies are working hard to teach people how to keep themselves healthy.

Europe and . . .

Western Europe is doing everything it can to teach people how to keep themselves safe from the HIV virus. People there can take HIV medicines, and not so many people are dying.

Eastern Europe, however, is not doing as well. Many new countries in that part of the world are struggling to build their governments and businesses. HIV puts an added strain on them that is hard for them to handle.

Australia realized it had a problem with AIDS earlier than many parts of the world, and it did something about it more quickly. It has one of the best *programs* in the world for teaching about HIV/AIDS. That's why it has fewer new cases of HIV.

Australia

Words to Know

Programs: plans of action, sets of actions with a single goal.

South America

AIDS is a serious problem in South America, just as it is in the rest of the world. Brazil, the largest nation in South America, is fighting hard against HIV/AIDS, though.

One of the things Brazil does is hand out clean hypodermic needles for free. The government is also teaching its people other ways to protect themselves. And HIV drugs are cheap in Brazil, so that everyone can afford to be treated.

Not everyone in the world approves of Brazil's approach to AIDS. Some people think it's not fair to the companies that make the medicines if Brazil sells the medicine so cheaply. Other people say that by handing out clean needles, the government is saying it's okay to do drugs. But Brazil says the most important thing is keeping people safe and healthy.

What Is the World Doing to Fight AIDS?

Words to Know

Solidarity: agreement and support between people.

All over the world, AIDS is touching the lives of human beings, people not so different from you. And now people all over the world are joining the fight against AIDS.

Most of these people have names you've probably never heard—but many of them are famous people who use their position to bring more attention to the cause they've taken on. From the ordinary people who take part in AIDS marathons (like the one shown here) to hip-hop artists and fashion models, movie stars to talk show hosts, more and more people are getting involved. The red ribbon has become the symbol that stands for people's *solidarity* with all those who are living with HIV/AIDS.

Research

Scientific research is one of the strongest weapons in the battle against AIDS. Scientists are working hard to find new ways to treat HIV and slow its growth so people can live longer, healthier lives. Scientists are also trying to create a *vaccine* against HIV, so that people could get a shot and never have to worry about getting this disease. And most of all, scientists are hoping to someday find a way to completely cure HIV/AIDS, so people will no longer have to die from this terrible disease.

Research takes lots of money. The scientists who work on this problem need to be paid. Their equipment and materials are expensive. And their job takes lots of time. There aren't any easy, quick answers!

Some organizations are helping to raise money for AIDS research. Many people believe governments should be spending more on research so scientists can finally find a cure.

The United Nations

Words to Know

Millennium: a period of a thousand years. The year 2000 was the beginning of a new millennium.

Summit: a meeting between government leaders.

In September 2000, 189 of the world's nations met for the United Nations' *Millennium Summit*. One of the goals they set themselves was to fight HIV/AIDS. The United Nations set up a special group to do this job called UNAIDS, and in June 2011, the world met again to see how well UNAIDS was doing at meeting these goals:

- keeping HIV from spreading
- getting care and support to people who already have the virus
- working to make people and communities stronger, so they won't be as likely to get HIV
- helping countries cope with the costs of HIV/AIDS (both in terms of money and in human life)

Did You Know?

The World Health Organization (its headquarters in Geneva, Switzerland, is shown to the left) is the part of the United Nations that works especially with anything that has to do with health.

The United Nations began in 1945 as a group of countries that got together to work for the peace and well-being of the entire world.

(PRODUCT) RED

One of the stars who's leading the battle against AIDS is Bono from the rock group U2. In 1986, Bono went to Ethiopia, a country in Africa. There Bono was faced with thousands of sick and hungry people. As Bono talked to these people, he felt angry that they had to live like that. Today, he's still angry, and he uses his anger to make himself fight hard against AIDS. Bono is famous around the world not only because he's a rock star, but also because he's someone who speaks out on behalf of those who are living with HIV/AIDS.

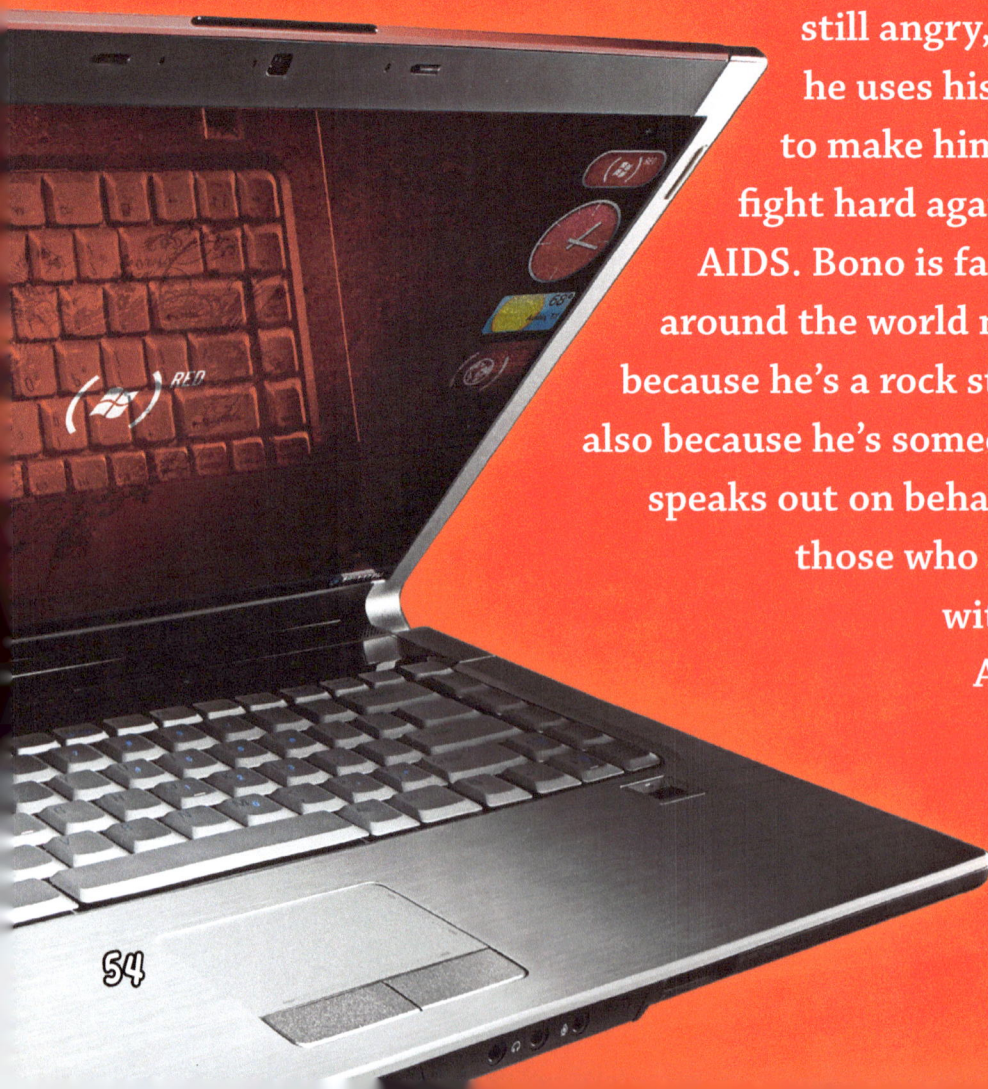

Bono doesn't just talk. He uses his position to take action. One thing he did was to help start a line of products called (PRODUCT) RED. These include everything from laptops to iPods®, T-shirts to jeans. A part of the sales from each of these products goes to the Global Fund, an organization that fights AIDS. Bono explained, "Now you're buying jeans and T-shirts, and you're paying for ten women in Africa to get medication for their children with HIV."

(From left to right) Bill Gates, Bono, and Michael Dell.

55

What Can You Do to Stay Safe?

The only way to be sure you won't catch HIV/AIDS is to protect yourself from other people's body fluids.

Sex is the way most people come into contact with body fluids, and condoms can help protect them.

Also be careful not to touch another person's sores or blood.

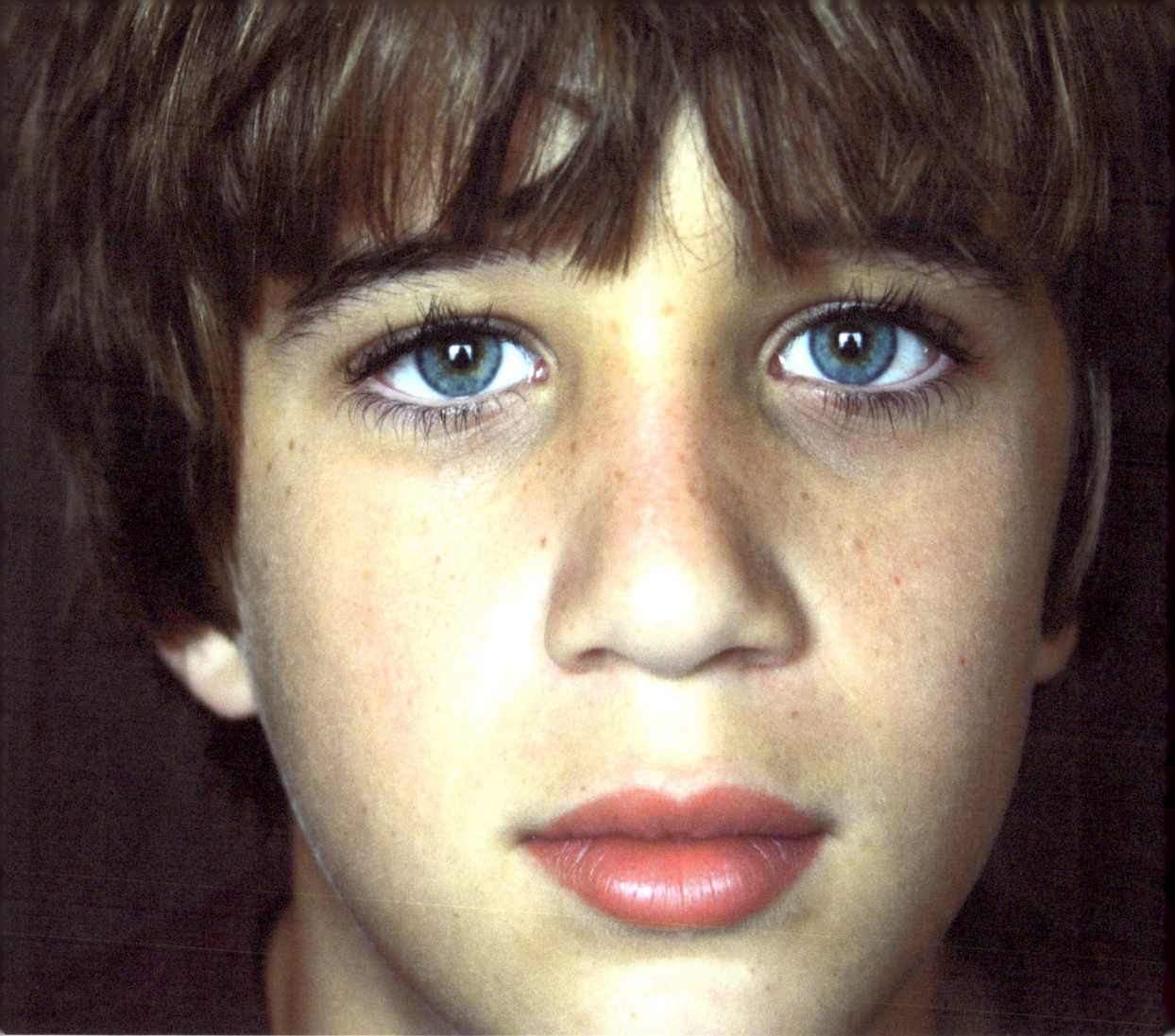

Pass the word. Tell your friends what they can do to stay safe. And join the people who are fighting HIV/AIDS. Do whatever you can!

Real Kids

Ryan White began 1984 as an ordinary thirteen-year-old. He had hemophilia, but it was being treated. He went to school and had friends, just like most kids his age. Then Ryan and his family found out he had caught HIV through the blood he had been given to treat his hemophilia. The HIV had already turned into AIDS. Doctors told Ryan and his family that he only had six months to live.

Ryan wanted to spend the last months of his life doing what he had been doing, going to school and being with friends. But the school didn't want him there. People were afraid Ryan's illness might "rub off" on the other students.

Ryan's battle to be allowed to attend school made news first in the United States and then around the world. Because of Ryan, people all over the world started thinking about AIDS.

On April 8, 1990, Ryan White lost his battle with AIDS. He had lived a lot longer than doctors thought he would, but he was only nineteen when he died. Still, he had done a lot with his life. Because he fought hard to make people realize that AIDS is a problem we must all face, laws were passed to help people with HIV/AIDS. Television shows were made. Magazine articles were written, and education programs were started in schools. The world began to work together to fight this terrible disease—all because one young boy was brave enough to take a stand.

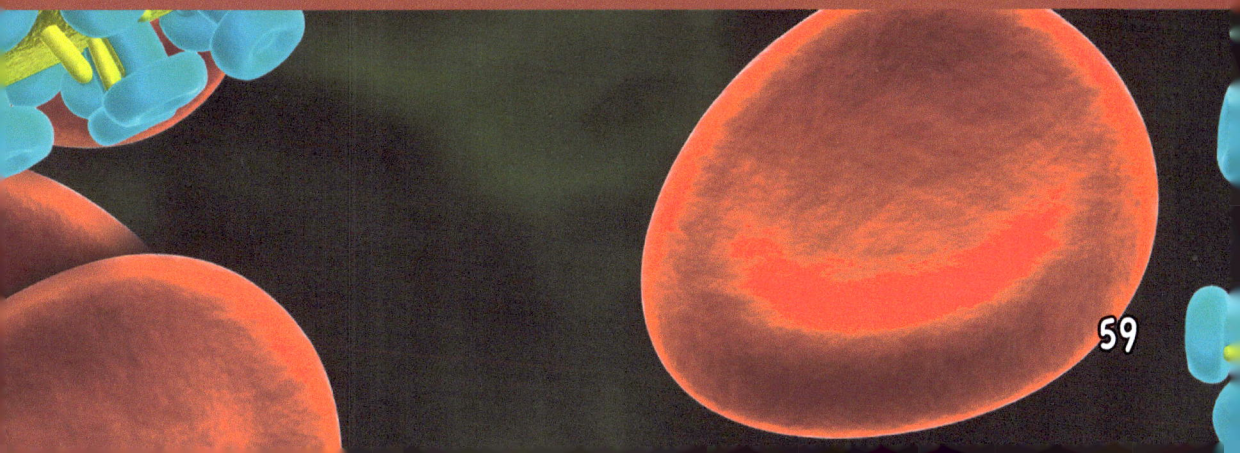

Find Out More

These websites will tell you more about HIV/AIDS, what you can do to protect yourself, and how you can help fight this disease.

eSchoolToday.com: AIDS and HIV
eschooltoday.com/hiv-aids/hiv-aids-introduction.html

HIV and AIDS
www.kidshealth.org/kid/health_problems/infection/hiv.html

Kids Talk AIDS
www.kidstalkaids.org/program/index.html

Let's Talk: Children, Families, and HIV
www.kidstalkaids.org/education/index.html

Talking with Kids: HIV and AIDS
www.talkwithkids.org/aids.html

Index

acupuncture 35
Africa 12, 40–42 54, 55
aloe 35
alternative medicine 35
antibodies 17, 30

bacteria 17, 51
B-cells 17
blood 7, 12, 15, 17, 22–23, 25, 28, 30–31, 43, 56, 58
Bono 54–55
Brazil 46–47

chimpanzee 12
cure 32, 34, 50–51

developed countries/nations 32, 36, 37
  Europe 36–37, 44
disease 5, 7–11, 15, 17, 22, 26–27, 40–42, 50–51, 59–60
drug 24, 25, 34, 46–47

hemophilia 23, 58
hospital 22, 36
hypodermic 24, 46

immune system 7, 9, 15, 35, 51
India 42–43
infection 15, 17, 31, 60

Japan 36

medicine 27, 32, 34–37, 39, 41, 44, 47, 62, 64

needles 24–25, 28–29, 35, 46–47
North America 37–38

pregnancy 27
(PRODUCT) RED 54, 55

Red Cross 22
research 50–51
Russia 42

sexual intercourse 20
South America 46
St. John's Wort 35

tattoo 28–29
T Cells 17, 31

United Nations, The 52–53

vaccine 7, 50–51
virus 7, 10, 11, 12, 17, 22, 25–27, 30, 32, 41, 44, 51, 53

White, Ryan 58, 59

Picture Credits

About the Author

Rae Simons has written many books for young adults and children. She lives with her family in New York State in the U.S.

About the Consultant

Elise DeVore Berlan, MD, MPH, FAAP, is a faculty member of the Division of Adolescent Health at Nationwide Children's Hospital and an assistant professor of Clinical Pediatrics at the Ohio State University College of Medicine. She completed her fellowship in Adolescent Medicine at Children's Hospital Boston and obtained a master's degree in public health at the Harvard School of Public Health. Dr. Berlan completed her residency in pediatrics at the Children's Hospital of Philadelphia, where she also served an additional year as chief resident. She received her medical degree from the University of Iowa College of Medicine.

www.ingramcontent.com/pod-product-compliance
Lightning Source LLC
Chambersburg PA
CBHW042017080426

42735CB00002B/79